W9-CEV-452

EXTREME SURVIVAL IN THE MILITARY

SURVIVING BY TRAPPING, FISHING, & EATING PLANTS

EXTREME SURVIVAL IN THE MILITARY

Learning Mental Endurance for Survival

Ropes & Knots for Survival

Survival at Sea

Survival Equipment

Survival First Aid

Survival in the Wilderness

Surviving by Trapping, Fishing, & Eating Plants

Surviving Captivity

Surviving Hostage Rescue Missions

Surviving Natural Disasters

Surviving the World's Extreme Regions:
Desert, Arctic, Mountains, & Jungle

Surviving with Navigation & Signaling

EXTREME SURVIVAL IN THE MILITARY

SURVIVING BY TRAPPING, FISHING, & EATING PLANTS

PATRICK WILSON

Introduction by Colonel John T. Carney. Jr., USAF-Ret.
President, Special Operations Warrior Foundation

MASON CREST

Mason Crest
450 Parkway Drive, Suite D
Broomall, PA 19008
www.masoncrest.com

Printed and bound in the United States of America

10 9 8 7 6 5 4 3 2 1

Series ISBN: 978-1-4222-3081-7
ISBN: 978-1-4222-3088-6
ebook ISBN: 978-1-4222-8780-4

Cataloging-in-Publication Data on file with the Library of Congress.

Picture Credits
Ardea: 13, 22, 32, 34, 36, 40, 42/43, 46, 48; **Corbis:** 14, 27, 55; **TRH:** 6, 11, 24, 52, 53; **Military Picture Library:** 8, 16, 50; **US Dept. of Defense:** 37
Illustrations courtesy of Amber Books and De Agostini UK

ACKNOWLEDGMENT
For authenticating this book, the Publishers would like to thank the Public Affairs Offices of the U.S. Special Operations Command, MacDill AFB, FL.; Army Special Operations Command, Fort Bragg, N.C.; Navy Special Warfare Command, Coronado, CA.; and the Air Force Special Operations Command, Hurlbert Field, FL.

IMPORTANT NOTICE
The survival techniques and information described in this publication are for educational use only. The publisher is not responsible for any direct, indirect, incidental or consequential damages as a result of the uses or misuses of the techniques and information within.

DEDICATION
This book is dedicated to those who perished in the terrorist attacks of September 11, 2001, and to the Special Forces soldiers who continually serve to defend freedom.

CONTENTS

Introduction   7

Hunting and Trapping Animals   9

Fishing   23

Edible Plants   33

Cooking   51

Series Glossary of Key Terms   60

Equipment Requirements   61

Useful Websites   62

Further Reading/About the Author   63

Index   64

KEY ICONS TO LOOK FOR:

Text-Dependent Questions: These questions send the reader back to the text for more careful attention to the evidence presented there.

Words to Understand: These words with their easy-to-understand definitions will increase the reader's understanding of the text, while building vocabulary skills.

Series Glossary of Key Terms: This back-of-the book glossary contains terminology used throughout this series. Words found here increase the reader's ability to read and comprehend higher-level books and articles in this field.

Research Projects: Readers are pointed toward areas of further inquiry connected to each chapter. Suggestions are provided for projects that encourage deeper research and analysis.

Sidebars: This boxed material within the main text allows readers to build knowledge, gain insights, explore possibilities, and broaden their perspectives by weaving together additional information to provide realistic and holistic perspectives.

INTRODUCTION

Elite forces are the tip of Freedom's spear. These small, special units are universally the first to engage, whether on reconnaissance missions into denied territory for larger, conventional forces or in direct action, surgical operations, preemptive strikes, retaliatory action, and hostage rescues. They lead the way in today's war on terrorism, the war on drugs, the war on transnational unrest, and in humanitarian operations as well as nation building. When large scale warfare erupts, they offer theater commanders a wide variety of unique, unconventional options.

Most such units are regionally oriented, acclimated to the culture and conversant in the languages of the areas where they operate. Since they deploy to those areas regularly, often for combined training exercises with indigenous forces, these elite units also serve as peacetime "global scouts" and "diplomacy multipliers," a beacon of hope for the democratic aspirations of oppressed peoples all over the globe.

Elite forces are truly "quiet professionals": their actions speak louder than words. They are self-motivated, self-confident, versatile, seasoned, mature individuals who rely on teamwork more than daring-do. Unfortunately, theirs is dangerous work. Since "Desert One"—the 1980 attempt to rescue hostages from the U.S. embassy in Tehran, for instance—American special operations forces have suffered casualties in real world operations at close to fifteen times the rate of U.S. conventional forces. By the very nature of the challenges which face special operations forces, training for these elite units has proven even more hazardous.

Thus it's with special pride that I join you in saluting the brave men and women who volunteer to serve in and support these magnificent units and who face such difficult challenges ahead.

Colonel John T. Carney, Jr., USAF-Ret.
President, Special Operations Warrior Foundation

When preparing a snare, you should try to disguise your human smell by smearing your hand with mud or covering the snare with ash.

WORDS TO UNDERSTAND

effective: Able to do a job easily and quickly.

unrestricted: Not limited or blocked.

vegetation: Plants.

carcass: Dead body.

domestic: Tamed.

aggressive: Ready or likely to attack.

nutritious: Containing things that are needed to keep the human body healthy.

HUNTING AND TRAPPING ANIMALS

No matter where elite troops are, they can always find food for survival. There are many types of plant and animal foods available. Soldiers are trained where to find them, how to recognize them, and how to collect or trap them. They must also know what is poisonous and dangerous.

To be fit and to have enough energy, soldiers need more than 3,000 to 5,000 calories a day in warm weather and 4,000 to 6,000 calories a day in cold climates.

They must try to eat a balanced diet to keep their body and mind working properly. The four main elements to a balanced diet, which they should eat on a daily basis, are:

- Protein. This is essential for growth and repair of tissue. Protein is broken down into amino acids, which are important for muscular growth and repair. Protein is found in cheese, milk, cereal grains, fish, meat, and poultry.
- Carbohydrates. These are the body's main source of energy. They should make up about half of the daily calorie intake. Carbohydrates can be obtained from fruit, vegetables, chocolate, milk, and cereal grains.

A deadfall trap is very effective, but can easily be set off and can kill humans as well as animals. Always remember where you set them.

- Fats. They provide the greatest source of energy. Fats are used by the body when it has used up its carbohydrate store. Fats can be obtained from butter, cheese, oils, nuts, egg yolks, margarine, and animal fats.

- Minerals and vitamins. These are important for keeping a person fit and providing a well-balanced diet.

Animals as food

Troops always remember one thing about getting food from animals: never to use more energy getting the food than they receive from it once they have caught and cooked it. Elite soldiers are trained to be skilled in hunting and trapping. They learn about the types of animals that inhabit the area they are in, their tracks, habits, and where they sleep.

The best animals for flavor and quantity of meat are mature females, but all animals will provide a soldier with meat of one kind or another. If soldiers do not have a gun, they will kill animals using snares and traps. Most of what they catch in this way will be small animals and birds.

If they do have guns, they observe the following rules when hunting prey:

- Walk as quietly as possible.
- Move slowly, stop frequently, and listen.
- Be observant; hunt upwind or crosswind whenever possible so the prey is not alerted to your presence.
- Try to blend in with the terrain features.
- Be prepared. Game often startles hunters and catches them off guard, resulting in a badly aimed shot.
- Make the first shot count.

An elite soldier stalks through the jungle. Before stalking animals, human odor can be masked by standing in the smoke of a fire.

MAKE CONNECTIONS: CANADIAN FORCES' HUNTING TIPS

Canada's Special Forces troops are very good at locating animals for food in the frozen parts of their country by being alert and aware of animal habits. They look for:

- Trails beaten down by heavy use.
- Tracks, which can provide information on the type, size, age, and sex of animals.
- Droppings, a good indicator of animal type and size.
- Feeding grounds and water holes, good sites for hunting in the early morning or evening.
- Dens, holes, and food stores, good sites for setting traps.

Elite troops are trained to set traps correctly in order to catch animals. The following traps are all **effective**.

Snares

A snare is a wire or string loop placed in such a way that an animal is forced to put its head through it. The snare will then tighten, thus killing the animal (although not always immediately).

If an elite soldier is setting snares, he or she checks them regularly. It is unfortunate that a snare designed to strangle one type of animal may sometimes catch another by a leg and not kill it immediately. In this case, the animal may bite off its own limb to escape, or attract the attention of

Troops use animal footprints to help them track down prey. Fresh dung and droppings can also indicate that animals are close by.

another predator and be killed and taken away before the soldier can get to the trap. Either way, always check snares for trapped animals and ensure that they are working. Soldiers cannot afford to let any prey escape their grasp.

The elite Special Forces are taught how to catch animals with a minimum of effort. They learn that it is far better to work with nature than against it. This means setting traps where animals will walk into them, and obeying the following rules:

- Make sure the traps are working properly.
- Check them regularly.
- Do not walk on animal trails.
- Always lay traps on trails that the animals use regularly.
- Place a snare so that, when an animal is caught, it will be lifted off the ground.

- Approach any animal caught in a snare with caution.
- Use fish entrails as bait.
- Position foliage in such a way that it will force animals to pass through the snares.

The size of the loop needed to catch certain animals and the height of the snare is shown opposite:

Animal	Diameter	Height above trail
Hare	4 inches (10 cm)	3 inches (7.5 cm)
Squirrel	3 inches (7.5 cm)	1½ inches (3.75 cm)
Rabbit	4 inches (10 cm)	2 inches (5 cm)
Wolf	16 inches (40 cm)	17½ inches (43.75 cm)

The size of trap required to snare this fox will be bigger than that required to catch a rabbit, hare or squirrel.

Positioning snares

Soldiers have a number of aims when positioning snares which they must adhere to if they are to trap their prey successfully. They must keep the loop open and **unrestricted** so it can tighten on the animal, and keep it a proper distance off the ground. They should site snares on heavily used trails, in an area where animals are feeding on **vegetation** or on a **carcass**, or near a den or store of food they regularly visit.

Snaring a main trail is called a "trail set" and is an effective way of catching animals. Troops remember that animals are creatures of habit. They will stick to well-worn trails.

Deadfall traps

The principle of these traps is simple: when the bait is taken, a weight falls on the prey and kills it. There are many types of deadfall triggers, but they are all activated either by a tripline release action or a baited release action.

With the tripline release, the animal touches or trips a line, stick, or pole, activating the deadfall. With the baited release, the animal is attracted by the bait, and when it pulls on it, the deadfall will drop.

Spear traps

These traps can be very effective. They consist of a spring that is held in place by a tripline, with a spear being fixed firmly to the springy shaft, which hits the animal when released.

Elite forces warning: these traps can kill humans. Troops always approach them from behind.

Elite troops setting a figure-four trigger deadfall trap. The animal will be killed by a weight falling onto it.

Bird traps

There are several effective ways of catching birds. An extremely simple method is for a soldier to put a stone in a piece of bait and to throw it into the air. A bird will attempt to swallow it, but the stone will catch in its mouth, causing it to fall to earth, whereupon the soldier can club it.

The following traps will also serve soldiers well.

- Suspended snares: troops hang a line of snares across a stream above water level.

- Baited hooks: fish hooks buried in fruit or other food are a good way of catching birds. The hooks catch in the birds' throats.

- Noose sticks: elite soldiers tie a number of nooses (half to one inch/1.25- 2.5 cm in diameter) close together along a branch or stick. They then place the stick in a favorite roosting or nesting spot. Birds become entangled when they alight.

A spear trap. When the animal trips the wire, the spring-loaded branch is released, which drives the spear into the animal.

Trapping animals

Mammals can be a valuable food source for the survivor. They are divided into the following groups.

Wild cats

They range in size from **domestic**-sized cats to lions and tigers. Troops avoid the big cats unless they have a gun. The smaller ones can be caught with powerful spring snares.

Wild dogs

They can be caught with snares, though they have a nasty bite. Troops are always careful when it comes to dealing with wild dogs. They can be very **aggressive**.

Bears

Bears are best avoided. These big, strong creatures can outrun a horse over short distances and can kill a person easily. Soldiers also keep away from bear cubs (the mother bear will be nearby). They know too that a wounded bear will be extremely angry, and very dangerous. Soldiers hunt a bear only if they have guns. They must make sure they kill with the first shot to the brain. Bears can also be killed using a spear trap. It is important for soldiers to be sure that the trap will kill. Bears are not therefore an easy food source.

Weasels, stoats, mink, martens, and polecats

Troops must be careful because these animals have sharp teeth. They can be caught by spring snares and deadfalls.

**MAKE CONNECTIONS:
LIVING FROM THE LAND**

Elite troops spend many months on survival exercises. This provides them with an invaluable understanding of different terrains, and the food that can be found in these areas. They must learn to fend for themselves.

Wolverines

Wolverines are badger-shaped animals. They should only be tackled face to face by a soldier armed with a gun. They can be caught from a distance using spring snares.

Badgers

They have a fierce bite. They can be caught in spring snares and deadfall traps.

Cattle

Large cattle, especially bulls, can be dangerous. Because they are especially large animals, soldiers need very powerful snares, spring traps, and deadfalls to kill cattle.

Deer and antelopes

Troops need to beware of their horns. They can gouge and stab and inflict serious wounds. The small types can be caught in snares and deadfalls, and the larger ones by spear traps and larger deadfalls.

TEXT-DEPENDENT QUESTIONS

1. List three rules to follow when hunting.
2. What are three different kinds of traps?
3. Explain how a deadfall trap works.
4. Why should bears usually be avoided?

Wild pigs

The tusks of a wild pig can cause serious injury. Wild pigs can be caught with strong spring snares, deadfalls, and pig spear traps.

Rodents and rabbits

These are easily caught with snares and spring snares.

Reptiles

These can be a valuable food source, but some can be extremely dangerous and are best left alone: crocodiles, alligators, gila monsters, and beaded lizards. Elite soldiers never eat toads—they have toxic skin secretions.

Snakes

Troops treat all snakes as dangerous and poisonous, even if they are not. In order to kill a snake or protect themselves against it, they use a forked stick to pin it down just behind the head. The back of the head is then clubbed with another stick. Better still, they cut off the head with a machete. Elite soldiers

RESEARCH PROJECT

This chapter lists thirteen groups of animals that soldiers may hunt for food. Using either the library or the Internet, find out where each of these animals can be found. Label a map of the world with the kinds of animals that can be found in each region.

never pick up a snake until they are sure it is dead. Some snakes can look as if they are dead when they are not. Reflex actions can cause them to "bite" even after they are dead.

Snails, worms, and slugs

These are **nutritious**, but troops eat them only when they are fresh. They avoid snails with brightly colored shells since these are poisonous. They also avoid sea snails in tropical waters because some have stings that can kill. Worms should be starved for a day or squeezed between fingers to clear out muck.

WORDS TO UNDERSTAND

invaluable: Extremely useful.

filleting: Removing the bones from a fish.

internal: On the inside.

borehole: A deep, narrow hole made with a drill.

filaments: Threads or very slender fibers.

tendrils: Threadlike parts of plants that often grow in a spiral and twine around things for support.

shoals: Large groups of fish swimming together.

dinghy: A small, open boat.

potent: Having great power.

lethal: Able to cause death.

potentially: Having to do with the ability to become something else in the future.

estuaries: The areas where streams or rivers meet the ocean.

lagoons: Stretches of salt water separated from the sea by a sandbank or reef.

reefs: Ridges of rock, coral, or sand just below the surface of the sea.

FISHING

Fishing can be an invaluable aid to the survivor when it comes to finding food. There are fish in the seas, rivers, and lakes in all parts of the world, and they can be caught relatively easily. This is where the hooks and lead weights in an elite soldier's survival kit (see the Equipment Requirements on pages 61-62) are worth their weight in gold. He or she will employ the fishing methods listed below to catch fish.

Still fishing

Soldiers weight their lines with a float, lead weight, or a rock. They attach a baited hook and let it settle on the bottom of the river or float. Then they take up the slack and wait for a strike. Every once in a while they pull on the line.

Dry fly fishing

This method is used when fish feed off the surface of the water. Elite soldiers use a line with a stick, a length of string, or line. They cast the fly upstream and let it float down past them. Troops are encouraged to experiment with the size and color of their flies. This method of fishing cannot be used in very cold weather when there are no airborne insects around because the fish will not bite.

Ice fishing. Troops make a hole in the ice to put lines through, usually with a signaling device, such as a handkerchief, attached.

Set lining

This involves casting a long line with several baited hooks into the water and leaving it overnight. A soldier normally puts out two lines, one on the bottom and one off the bottom.

Gill netting

This is done by setting out a net that is constructed to catch fish by their gills as they try to swim through it. It is very effective for streams. Stones are tied along the bottom edge of the net to keep it on the bottom. Alternatively, a soldier makes a trap with stones or rocks and herds fish into it.

Gutting a fish can be done very quickly, once you know how to do it. Fish are packed with nutrients, such as protein and B vitamins.

Filleting fish

The best method of **filleting** fish is to slit the fish from its tail to just behind the gills and pull out the **internal** organs (see next page). A soldier then washes and cleans the flesh, and trims off the fins and tail. After this, he cuts down to, but not through, the spine. The soldier then cuts around the spine, finishing behind the gills on both sides. He inserts his thumb along the top of the spine and begins to pull it away from the flesh. The ribs should come out cleanly with the spine.

Fishing in polar regions

Ice may be as much as 13 feet (4.5 m) thick, so elite soldiers need to choose an appropriate spot to create a **borehole** for fishing, where the ice is not too thick to make a hole but thick enough to take their weight. They can dangle a line on the end of a small stick with a signaling device attached to it, such as a handkerchief or piece of card. They tie this stick to another that is laid across the fishing hole. When a fish bites, it should cause the pennant to spring up.

You should not eat fish that have sunken eyes, slimy gills, flabby flesh or skin, or an unpleasant smell. All types of jellyfish should also be avoided.

A soldier should easily be able to find clams, crawfish, mussels, snails and limpets, chitons, sea urchins, and king crab on most Arctic shores. It is important not to eat dead shellfish. The small black purple mussel of the northern Pacific waters is poisonous and should be avoided. Kelp and other smaller seaweed are edible, though a soldier avoids seaweed that has long **filaments** and **tendrils**.

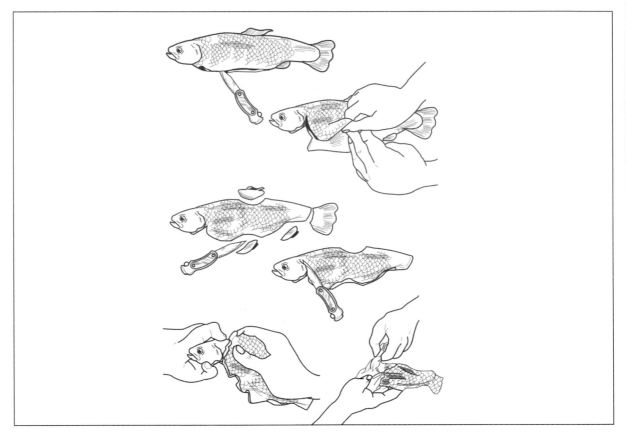

The process of filleting a fish. This method ensures that the ribs come out with the spine.

Fishing at sea

Fish are the obvious source of food at sea. They are high in protein, and require little body water to digest. Troops use the following tips for catching fish at sea:

- Protect your hands when holding a fishing line as well as when holding a fish.
- Use small fish as bait. These can be found by rigging up a net to catch them. They can also be used as food.
- Cut loose any over-large fish and do not fish if sharks are near.

- Try to head for large **shoals** of fish, but always be aware that shark and barracuda may also be present.
- Be careful not to puncture the **dinghy** with fish hooks or any other sharp object.
- Gut the fish immediately after catching them. Any fish that the survivor does not eat can be dried in the sun. But make sure you have enough water if you are going to eat dried fish.

As well as a fishing line, soldiers can also bind a knife to an oar to use as a spear to catch larger fish, though they should be wary. If the fish is too large, the weight of it might capsize the dinghy or cause it damage.

Here is a list of sea life that should be avoided.

Auger or tenebra shell

Dangerously poisonous. Similar to cone shells (see below), though narrower and with less **potent** poison.

Blue-ringed octopus

Deadly poisonous. Found mostly in the Australian barrier reef, they can be grayish white with blue, ringlike marks. All octopi can vary their color, so troops need to treat any tropical species with caution. Their bite can be **lethal**.

Cone shell

Deadly poisonous. Mainly found in warm tropical regions, the cone shell has a small opening at the narrow end of its body from which the snail can shoot out a poisonous needle. The venom can be **potentially** lethal.

Porcupine fish (right)

Poisonous. It is greenish with dark patches on the back, with spiky appearance over upper body and sides. Inflates into a ball when alarmed.

Portuguese man-of-war

Found mainly in tropical seas, but can drift across to European waters. Floating portion can be as small as 6 in (15 cm), but the tentacles can be 40 feet (12 m) long. The sting is painful but not usually fatal.

Puffer fish (left)

Poisonous. Mottled green with black spots. Inflates into a ball when alarmed.

Rabbitfish

Dangerously poisonous. Green, round, flattened shape, with sharp spines on their fins. It is about one foot (30 cm) in length. Although this fish is edible, the spines can cause intense pain.

Stingray

Dangerously poisonous. Found usually in warm, shallow water. They have a dark, diamond-shape appearance with a long, whiplike tail. The tail can inflict a serious wound. Stingrays are the most common cause of severe fish stings.

Stonefish

Deadly poisonous. Found in the shallow waters of the Pacific and Indian Oceans. They live among rocks and coral, and in mudflats and **estuaries**.

MAKE CONNECTIONS: ANTISHARK MEASURES

Troops of the U.S. Navy SEALs are experienced at operating within shark-infested waters. When confronted by sharks, the troops form a tight circle for added protection; they ward off an attack by kicking the sharks; and if a member of the team has a knife, he or she will aim for the snout, gills, or eyes. SEALs *never* swim away from sharks.

Because of their green color, they are very difficult to see. If stepped on, they can have an intensely painful and sometimes fatal sting.

Swordfish, marlin, sailfish, spearfish

These are all large fish with a spike or spear on the upper jaw. These fish are not normally dangerous but will react if attacked or wounded. Elite troops are taught to leave them alone because the spike could be lethal in a life raft.

Tang or surgeonfish

Dangerously poisonous. Flat and rounded, tropical water fish have bright blue and green colors. Troops should not be fooled by the pleasant appearance of this fish because the spines, especially in the tail, can inflict a painful sting.

TEXT-DEPENDENT QUESTIONS

1. What is set lining?
2. Explain gill netting.
3. Describe how to fillet a fish.
4. List several sea animals that should never be eaten.

Toadfish

Dangerously poisonous. They look like a cross between a toad and a fish, and lurk in mud in the winter. They can also be found in both shallow and deep water. They have sharp spines near the gills, and the first dorsal fin can inflict a painful sting.

Triggerfish

Poisonous. Can be dark with algae-like greenish patches on the side and underbelly.

Tuna

Potentially dangerous. A large tuna fish can bite the head off a dolphin. If soldiers are in a small craft, they will treat them with caution, even though tuna are good to eat.

RESEARCH PROJECT

Pick one of the sea animals mentioned in this chapter and find out more about it. Do a search on the Internet and consult library books to answer these questions:

• In what regions is this creature found?

• How big is it?

• What areas of the sea does it prefer?

• Why is it dangerous?

Can you find any news stories about someone being injured or poisoned by this sea creature? Print pictures from the Internet or draw your own illustrations to show what this animal looks like.

Weeverfish

Dangerously poisonous. Long-bodied fish, about one foot (30 cm) in length, which tend to bury themselves in sand. Their mouths are large and slanted upward, with eyes on the top of their heads. They have poisonous spines in the fins, which deliver a painful sting.

As a general rule, troops are careful of fish that inhabit **lagoons** and **reefs**, and in particular of fish with small mouths and small belly fins.

WORDS TO UNDERSTAND

mission: A military task or job.

geographic: Having to do with the Earth's physical
features—such as mountains, rivers, oceans, etc.—
as well as how these features are used by humans.

constituents: Parts.

irritation: Soreness or itchiness.

inflammation: A condition when part of the body becomes hot,
swollen, and sore.

decomposing: Rotting.

EDIBLE PLANTS

There are thousands of edible plants available throughout the world. Before going on a mission, the elite soldier will have learned about the geographic area in which he or she is working. Some of the most common edible plants are listed in this chapter.

When selecting unknown plants to eat, soldiers must carry out the taste test to see if they are safe to eat. It is important to test all parts of the plant—many plants have one or more edible parts.

The U.S. Army has a simple test for establishing whether a plant is safe to eat, called the Universal Edibility Test. It cannot be applied to mushrooms and other fungi. The test works as follows:

- Test only one part of the plant at a time.
- Break the plant into its base **constituents**: leaves, stem, and roots.
- Smell the plant for strong or acid odors.
- Do not eat for eight hours before starting the test.
- During this time put a sample of the plant on the inside of the elbow or wrist. Fifteen minutes is enough time for a reaction to develop.
- During the test period, take nothing by mouth except pure water and the plant being tested.
- Select a small portion of the component.
- Before putting it in the mouth, place the plant piece on the outer surface of the lip to test for burning or itching.

Edible plants are plentiful in the jungle—but so are poisonous ones. To be safe, troops will carry out the Universal Edibility Test.

Sweet potatoes—a tropical climbing plant—are an excellent natural food source. They are rich in starch, and can be roasted or boiled.

- If, after three minutes, there is no reaction, place it on the tongue and hold it there for 15 minutes.
- If there is no reaction, chew a piece thoroughly and hold it in the mouth for 15 minutes. Do not swallow.
- If there is no **irritation** whatsoever during this time, swallow the food.
- Wait for eight hours. If any ill effects occur, try to vomit and drink plenty of water.

   If no bad effects occur, eat half a cup of the same plant prepared the same way. Wait another eight hours. If no ill effects are suffered, the plant as prepared is safe to eat.

Edible underground parts of plants

Tubers (the short, rounded rootlike part of a stem), usually found below ground, are rich in starch and are eaten roasted or boiled. Plants with edible tubers include arrowhead, tara, yam, cattail, and chufa.

Roots and rootstalks are rich in starch. Plants with edible rootstalks include baobab, goa bean, water plantain, bracken, reindeer moss, cow parsnip, wild calla, rock tripe, canna lily, cattail, chicory, horseradish, tree fern, lotus lily, angelica, and water lily.

Death camas is a poisonous bulb that has white or yellow flowers. However, other bulbs are edible, including wild lily, wild tulip, wild onion, blue camas, and tiger lily.

Edible shoots grow in much the same way as asparagus. Many can be eaten raw, but they are better boiled. Edible shoots include purslane, reindeer moss, bamboo, fishtail palm, goa bean, bracken, rattan, wild rhubarb, cattail, sago palm, rock tripe, papaya, sugar cane, and lotus lily.

Plants with edible leaves

These are perhaps the most numerous of all edible plants and include dandelion, fireweed, dock, mountain sorrel, and nettle. In addition, the young tender leaves of nearly all nonpoisonous plants are edible.

Some plants with edible leaves have an edible pith in the center of the stem. Examples include buri, fishtail, sago, coconut, rattan, and sugar cane.

The inner barks of a tree (the layer next to the wood) may be eaten raw by troops. However, they avoid the outer bark, which contains large amounts of bitter tannin (chemical residue from trees).

Flower parts

Edible flowers include abal, wild rose, colocynth, papaya, banana, horseradish, wild caper, and luffa sponge. Pollen has the appearance of yellow dust and is high in food value.

Fruits and Vegetables

There are many kinds of edible fruits, both of the sweet and non-sweet (vegetable) type. Sweet fruits include crab apple, wild strawberry, wild cherry, blackberry, crowberry, and cranberry. Vegetables include breadfruit, horseradish, rowan, and wild caper.

Cherries are a popular edible fruit with elite troops. Like most fruit, they are readily available in the wild.

A U.S. soldier shows one of a variety of edible plants to members of the Chilean Air Force during survival training in Santiago.

Seeds and grains

The grains of all cereals and other grasses are good sources of plant protein. They can be ground up and mixed with water to make cooked cereal. Plants with edible seeds and grains include amaranth, Italian millet, rice, bamboo, nipa palm, tamarind, screw pine, water lily, and purslane.

Nuts

Nuts are a good source of protein. Most can be eaten raw, though some, such as acorns, are better when cooked. Plants with edible nuts include almond, water chestnut, beechnut, oak, pine, chestnut, cashew, hazelnut, and walnut.

Pulps

In many fruits, the pulp around the seeds is the only edible part. Plants that produce edible pulp include the custard apple, inga pod, breadfruit, and tamarind.

Gums and resins

These are saps that collect and harden on the outside surface of the plant. Both are nutritious food sources, but beware of milky saps (see box below).

 MAKE CONNECTIONS: US AIR FORCE TIPS FOR EATING PLANTS

The U.S. Air Force has guidelines, drawn up for downed pilots, when selecting plants for possible consumption in the wild. They serve pilots well in a survival situation.

- Avoid plants with umbrella-shaped flowers, though carrots, celery, and parsley (all edible) are members of this family.
- Avoid all legumes (beans and peas); they absorb minerals from the soil and cause digestive problems.
- If in doubt, avoid all bulbs.
- Avoid all white and yellow berries—they are poisonous; half of all red berries are poisonous; blue or black berries are generally safe to eat.
- Single fruits on a stem are considered safe to eat.
- A milky sap indicates a poisonous plant.
- Plants that are irritants to the skin should not be eaten.

Saps

Vines and other plants may be tapped as potential sources of usable liquid. The flower stalk is cut and the fluid is drained into a container. It is highly nutritious. Plants with edible sap and drinking water include the following:

- Sweet acacia, colocynth, agave, saxual, rattan palm, cactus, and grape all contain water.
- Coconut palm, fishtail palm, sago palm, sugar palm, and buri palm all contain sap.

Poisonous plants

Elite soldiers will have knowledge of the most common types of poisonous plants so they can avoid them. In particular, they learn to identify hemlock and water hemlock, two of the deadliest.

Water Hemlock

Appearance: purple-streaked stems, small two- to three-lobed, toothed leaflets, and clusters of small white flowers.

Location: always found near water throughout the world.

Smell: unpleasant odor. Deadly

Hemlock

Appearance: up to six feet (2 m) high, multibranched. Hollow, purple-spotted stems, coarsely toothed leaves, lighter below. Thick clusters of tiny white flowers and white roots.

Location: grassy waste places throughout the world.

Smell: unpleasant odor. Deadly.

Elite troops avoid hemlock at all times. It is very poisonous but, with its unpleasant smell, it is easily recognizable.

Poison ivy

Appearance: three-part variable leaves, greenish flowers, and white berries. It causes poisoning through contact with the skin; in other words, it is a "contact poison."

Location: wooded areas of North America. Mildly poisonous.

Baneberry

Appearance: leaves made up of several toothed leaflets. Small, white flowers clustered at the end of a stem, with white or black berries.

Location: mostly in woodland areas. Mildly poisonous.

Poison sumac

Appearance: hairless, dark-spotted smooth bark, and clusters of white berries. It is a contact poison.

Location: swamplands of southeastern North America. Mildly poisonous.

Death camas

Appearance: long, straplike leaves, and loose clusters of greenish white, six-part flowers.

Location: grassy, rocky, and lightly wooded areas. Deadly.

Thorn-apple or jimson weed

Appearance: jagged-edged oval leaves; single large, trumpet-shaped white flower; and spiny fruit.

Location: most temperate areas, also tropics.

Smell: sickly odor. Deadly.

Foxgloves

Appearance: basal leaves topped by a tall, leafy spike of purple, pink, or yellow tube-shaped flowers.

Location: wastelands throughout the world. Very poisonous.

Monkshood

Appearance: leafy with palm-shaped, deeply segmented leaves and hairy, hoodlike purplish blue or yellow flowers.

Location: damp woods and in shaded areas. Very poisonous.

Deadly nightshade

Appearance: oval leaves, single bell-shaped purplish or greenish flowers and shiny black berries.

Location: European woodlands and scrub. Very poisonous.

Buttercups

Appearance: glossy, waxy bright yellow flowers with five or more overlapping petals.

Location: temperate and arctic areas. Can cause severe **inflammation** of the intestinal tract.

Lupins

Appearance: small leaflets in a palm shape or radiating like the spokes of a wheel. Spikes of "pea-flowers": blue, violet, sometimes pink, white, or yellow.

Location: clearings and grassy places in temperate areas. Deadly.

Foxgloves, like hemlock, are very poisonous. They are found in wastelands throughout the world. Despite their colorful appearance, elite troops avoid eating them at all costs.

Vetches or locoweeds

Appearance: many small, spear-shaped leaflets in opposite pairs and showy spikes of five-petaled "pea-flowers": yellowish white, pink to lavender, and purplish.

Location: grassland and mountain meadows. Very poisonous.

Larkspur

Appearance: leaflets sticking out like the spokes of a wheel. It has dark purple or blue flowers.

Location: moist areas. Very poisonous.

Deadly nightshade is a plant that grows mainly in Europe. It is poisonous and must be avoided at all times.

Henbane

Appearance: sticky hairs, toothed oval leaves. Creamy flowers streaked purple.

Location: bare ground, often found near sea.

Smell: bad odor. Deadly.

Nightshade berries

Appearance: berries ripen from green to black, red, yellow, or white. Plants are bushy, leaves usually long-stalked and spear-shaped. Avoid.

Edible fungi

Not all fungus is poisonous or deadly. The following ground fungi can be eaten by the survivor.

Giant puffball

Appearance: looks like a large football. Around one foot (30 cm) wide, white and leathery, turning yellow with age.

Boletes

Appearance: brownish cap, swollen stem, and white flesh. Slippery Jack is similar.

Horn of plenty

Appearance: horn- or funnel-shaped. Has a rough, crinkly dark-brown cap, and a smooth, tapering gray stem.

Hedgehog fungus

Appearance: has spikes instead of gills or pores.

Chanterelle

Appearance: irregular orange or yellow cap.

Oyster mushroom

Appearance: Olive-colored cap when young, fades with age.

Underground fungi such as truffles can be found in woodland areas of Europe. Growing beneath the soil, they are whitish when young, becoming darker with age.

A giant puffball is easy to recognize and is a good, safe source of food for soldiers in survival situations.

Fungi grows in a variety of places, including the trunks and branches of trees. The following tree fungi can be eaten by the survivor.

Beefsteak fungus

Appearance: reddish above, pinkish below, and rough-textured; looks like a large tongue with bloodlike juice. Tastes bitter.

Brain fungus

Appearance: resembles a brain or coral.

The horn of plenty is another edible fungi that elite troops can eat without fear. It grows near the roots of trees.

Chicken-of-the-woods

Appearance: bright lemon or yellow.

Troops must be very careful when selecting fungi to eat. The British Special
Air Service (SAS) use the following tips for collecting fungi:
*   Avoid any fungi with white gills, a cuplike appendage at the base of the
    stem (volva), and stem rings.
*   Avoid any fungi that are **decomposing** or wormy.
*   Unless positively identified, avoid altogether.

Poisonous fungi

The following poisonous fungi are very dangerous.

Yellow staining mushroom

Appearance: shows a yellow stain when bruised, and is strongly yellow at the
base.
Smell: smells of **carbolic.** Avoid.

Destroying angel

Appearance: totally white, with a large volva, a scaly stem, and a cap up to five
inches (12.5 cm) across.
Smell: sweet and sickly odor. Deadly.

Death cap

Appearance: greenish olive cap up to five inches (12.5 cm) across, paler stem,
large volva, white gills, and flesh. Deadly.

TEXT-DEPENDENT QUESTIONS

1. Explain how to do the edibility test to find out if a plant is okay to eat.
2. What are tubers? List several examples.
3. What are some plant foods that provide protein?
4. What kind of sap indicates something that's poisonous?
5. List several poisonous plants.
6. What are five kinds of edible seaweed?

Fly agaric

Appearance: bright red cap flecked with white, large volva up to nine inches (22.5 cm) across. Deadly.

With its red cap and white flecks, the fly agaric, which is found in pine and birch woods in the fall, is easily spotted. It is also very poisonous.

RESEARCH PROJECT

Make your own book of edible and inedible plants. Look on the Internet for images of each of the plants described in this book. Print out the images and glue them into a notebook. Label each image and note whether or not it is edible. Describe where each plant can be found.

Panther cap

Appearance: brownish, white flecked cap up to three inches (7.5 cm) across, white gills, and two to three hooplike rings at base of stem. Deadly.

Leaden entoloma

Appearance: dull, grayish white, deeply convex cap up to six inches (15 cm) across. Yellowish gills turning salmon pink and firm white flesh.

Smell: like bitter almonds and radishes. Deadly.

Seaweed

Edible seaweed can be found in shallow waters anchored to the bottom of rocks, or can be found floating on the open seas. Sea lettuce is light green; kelp is olive green; sugar-wrack has long, flat yellow brown **fronds**; Irish moss is purple or green; dulse is purplish red; and lavers have red, purplish, or brown fronds.

COOKING

Once an elite forces soldier has trapped an animal, the next stage is to cook it; it is inadvisable to eat the food raw. The main types of cooking are boiling, frying, parching, baking, steaming, and roasting. Each of these can be employed in the wild.

Boiling

Food can be boiled in a metal container, in a rock with a hollow in it (not rocks that soak up water—they can explode and inflict serious injuries), and a hollowed-out piece of wood. (Hang wood over the fire and add hot rocks to the water and food.) Food can also be boiled in coconut shells, seashells, and half sections of bamboo.

Frying

Place a flat piece of rock on a fire. When it is hot, fry food on it.

Parching

This method works well with nuts. An elite soldier puts food in a container or on a rock and heats it slowly until it is scorched.

Baking

This can be done by making an oven from a pit under a fire, a closed container, or a wrapping of leaves or clay. Another method of baking is to line a pit with

British SAS soldiers roasting a rabbit over a fire. Rabbits can be tracked by looking for droppings, burrows, hair, and fur.

A common sight—boiling water in a metal mess tin. Troops add hot water to dried food packets or use it for hot drinks.

moisture-free stones and build a fire in the pit. As the fire burns down, the soldier scrapes the coals back, puts the covered container in, and covers this with a layer of coals and a thin layer of dirt. The food will then bake.

Steaming

Also done in a pit. The food is wrapped in large leaves or moss. A layer of food is placed in a coal-lined pit. Another layer of leaves and moss is added and the soldier continues alternating layers of wrapped food and leaves or moss until the pit is almost full. A stick is then pushed through the layers of food and leaves or moss before the pit is sealed with dirt.

Roasting

Done with a skewer or spit over an open fire. Good for cooking whole fowls or small animals.

British Special Air Service (SAS) soldiers are experts at turning even the most unlikely looking and seemingly inedible creature into a tasty and nutritious meal.

• Meat: this is cut into small cubes and boiled. Soldiers treat pork in warm climates with caution, and cook it for a longer time at higher temperatures.

Before cooking a bird, pluck the feathers, then remove the entrails (except for the craw, heart, and liver) and cut off the feet.

Wild pig is infested with worms and liver fluke, and venison is also prone to worms.

• Fish: usually germ-free if caught in fresh water, it is best stewed or wrapped in leaves and baked.

• Birds: these are boiled; young birds can be roasted.

• Reptiles and amphibians: these are gutted and cooked in their skins in hot embers; when the skin splits, the soldier discards it and then boils the meat. Snake heads are cut off before cooking—some have venom glands in their heads. Frogs are skinned (many have poisonous skins) and roasted on a stick.

• Turtles and tortoises: these are boiled until their shell comes off; the meat is cut off and cooked until tender.

• Shellfish: crabs, lobsters, shrimps, and crayfish are boiled to remove harmful organisms. All seafood spoils rapidly, so it is important for troops to cook it as soon as possible.

• Insects and worms: these can be boiled. Alternatively, they can be fried on hot rocks, crushed, and then ground into a powder to add to soups and stews.

Fire

Fire is extremely important for all soldiers. It is a great morale booster. It keeps them warm, dries their clothes, boils water, and can be used for signaling. It is

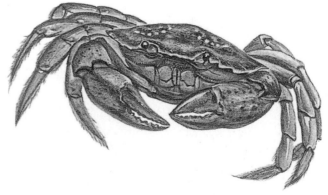

Crabs must be boiled before eating to remove bacteria.

also essential for cooking food. A member of the elite forces must therefore know how to build, start, and maintain a fire.

Making fire

The three ingredients of a successful fire are air, heat, and fuel. The key to making a fire is to prepare all the stages of the materials and ensure all the ingredients are present. Elite soldiers need to be patient and practice until they get it right. The materials for a fire fall into three categories: tinder, kindling, and fuel.

Tinder is any type of material that is easily lit. Soldiers are trained to use a variety of materials, including shredded tree bark, crushed leaves from dead

Ground fires are vital for sustaining the soldier while making camp. Handheld fire torches can also be used to deter dangerous animals.

plants, fine wood shavings, straw and grasses, sawdust, pitch wood shavings, discarded bird or rodent nest linings, seed down, charred cloth, cotton balls or lint, dry powdered sap from pine trees, dry paper, and foam rubber.

Elite soldiers get into the habit of always having tinder with them, and they remember to carry it in a waterproof container.

Kindling is then added to the tinder. It is used to bring the burning temperature of the fire up to the point where materials that burn less easily can be added. Kindling includes dead, small, dry twigs, coniferous seed cones and needles, and wood that has been doused with flammable materials.

Fuel does not have to be dry in order to burn, but moist wood will produce a lot of smoke. The best fuel sources are dry, dead wood, the insides of fallen trees, and large branches (which may be dry even if the outside is wet). Soldiers often split green wood and mix it with dry wood to be used as fuel. If there are no trees, troops are trained to use dead cactus, dry peat moss, or even dried animal manure.

MAKE CONNECTIONS: U.S. MARINES TIPS FOR FIREMAKING

Soldiers from the U.S. Marines use a simple set of rules for making and setting fires in the wild: They preserve their matches and always try to carry dry tinder in a waterproof container. In the arctic, they use a platform to prevent fire from melting down through deep snow and putting it out. In woods, they clear away ground debris to prevent the fire from spreading.

Gutting animals

After elite soldiers have killed an animal, they slit its throat to bleed it. The blood is saved if possible because it is full of vitamins and minerals. The carcass is then placed, belly up, on a slope.

Elite soldiers are trained to cut in a specific way. When they have caught the animal, they lay it on its back, then cut the skin on a straight line (it will help to have a sharp knife) from the tail bone to a point under the animal's neck. The skin is pressed open until the first two fingers can be inserted between the skin and the thin **membrane** enclosing the entrails. A knife blade is placed between the fingers, blade up, and the fingers forced forward, palm upward, cutting the skin but not the membrane.

On reaching the ribs, soldiers do not have to be as careful. They take away their fingers, force the knife under the skin, and lift. They will cut to a point at the bottom of the animal's chin. With the central cut completed, they make side cuts running between the right and left legs, across the belly, on both the front and hind. They cut up the inside of each leg to the knee and hock joints, before making cuts around the front legs just above the knees and around the hind legs above the hocks. The final cross is made across the chin, and then they cut completely around the neck and at the back of the ears. Now they begin skinning.

Skinning

This is begun at the corners where the cuts meet. After skinning the animal's side as far as possible, the soldier rolls the carcass onto its side to skin the back. Loose skin is spread out to prevent the meat from touching the ground

TEXT-DEPENDENT QUESTIONS

1. What is one danger of heating rocks in water?
2. Describe two methods of baking in the wild.
3. What are two ways that insects and worms can be eaten?
4. Why is being able to build a fire is so important to members of the elite forces?
5. Explain the difference between tinder and kindling.
6. What are two kinds of insects that you should not eat?

and the animal is turned on its skinned side. An elite soldier follows the same procedure on the opposite side until all the skin is free.

The entrails, heart, liver, and kidney can all be eaten, though the soldier discards any that are discolored. Blood is a good base for soups. Fat is good for making soups. Skin can be used as leather for clothing. **Tendons** and **ligaments** can be used for lashings. Bone marrow is a rich food source. Bones can be used for making tools and weapons.

Insects

All British SAS soldiers are taught how to catch and prepare insects to eat. These are the SAS instructions given to troops with regard to searching for insects:

• Be careful when searching for insects: their hiding places may also conceal scorpions, spiders, and snakes.

RESEARCH PROJECT

Eating insects can sound kind of yucky—but in other places of the world, people actually do eat these creatures regularly (not just when they are stranded in the wilderness). Use the Internet or library to discover which insects are most commonly eaten. What nutritional value do these insects offer? How are they cooked or prepared? Can you find a recipe for preparing an insect dish?

- Do not eat insects that have fed on manure: they carry infection.
- Do not eat brightly colored insects: they are poisonous.
- Do not collect grubs found on the underside of leaves: they secrete poisonous fluids.
- Avoid hornets' nests if at all possible: they guard their nests with vigor and their sting is vicious.
- Cook ants for at least six minutes to destroy the poisons that are found in some types.
- Boil all insects caught in water in case the water they were living in is polluted.

Elite troops avoid hornets' nests. Hornets have a nasty sting and it is best to stay well away from them.

SERIES GLOSSARY OF KEY TERMS

camouflage: Something that makes it hard to distinguish someone or something from the terrain or landscape around them.

casualty: A person who is killed or injured in a war or accident.

covert: Done in secret.

dehydrated: When you don't have enough water in your body for it to function properly. Alternatively, dehydrated food is food that has had all the water removed so that it won't go bad.

dislocation: When a joint is separated; when a bone comes out of its socket.

edible: Able to be eaten.

exposure: A health condition that results from bad weather around you. For example, when you get hypothermia or frostbite from cold weather, these are the results of exposure.

flares: A device that burns brightly, and can be used to signal for help. They can only be used once.

hygiene: The techniques and practices involved with keeping yourself clean and healthy.

improvised: Used whatever was available to make or create something. When you don't have professionally made equipment, you can make improvised equipment from the materials naturally found around you.

insulation: Something that keeps you warm and protects you from the cold.

kit: All of the clothing and equipment carried by a soldier.

layering: A technique of dressing for the wilderness that involves wearing many layers of clothing. If you become too warm or too cold, it is easy to remove or add a layer.

marine: Having to do with the ocean.

morale: Confidence, enthusiasm, and discipline at any given time. When morale is high, you are emotionally prepared to do something difficult. When morale is low, you might be angry, scared, or anxious.

purification: The process of making water clean and safe enough to drink.

terrain: The physical features of a stretch of land. Hard or rough terrain might be mountains or thick forests, and easy terrain would be an open field.

windbreak: Something that you use to block the wind from hitting you. If you camp somewhere exposed to the wind, it will be very difficult to stay warm.

EQUIPMENT REQUIREMENTS

Clothing and Shelter

Thermal underwear

Thin layer of synthetic material

Woolen or wool mixture shirt

Woven fiber sweater or jacket
  (normally a fleece)

Gore-Tex® jacket

At least two pairs of socks

Compact, light, windproof pants
  with numerous pockets and zippers
  to carry items securely.

Waterproof pants

Gloves—leather or mittens

Balaclava (woolen covering for head
  and face)

Spare clothing—socks, underwear,
  shirts etc.

Soft, well-maintained leather boots

H-frame knapsack, with side pockets

Portable, lightweight, waterproof
  shelter

A survival tin

Knife

Matches

Flint

Sewing kit

Water purification tablets

Compass

Mirror

Safety Pins

Wire

Plastic bag

Antiseptic cream

Snare wire

Survival bag

Pliers with wire cutter

Dental floss (for sewing)

Folding knife

Ring saw

Snow shovel

Signal cloth

Fishing hooks and flies

Weights and line

Multivitamins

Protein tablets

Large chocolate bar

Dried eggs

Dried milk

File

Cutlery set

Three space blankets

Four candles

Microlite flashlight

Extra battery and bulb

Fire starter

Windproof and waterproof matches

Butane lighter

Insect repellent

Snares

Plastic cup

Slingshot and ammunition

Knife sharpener

Whistle

Soap

Two orange smoke signals

A mess tin

Equipment for fishing

Net

Long line

Small bait

Fish hooks

Spear

Knife

Flies

Equipment for hunting and trapping

Rope

Tripline

Pole or stick

Snares

Noose sticks

Fish hooks

USEFUL WEBSITES

aggie-horticulture.tamu.edu/earthkind/landscape/poisonous-plants-resources/
    common-poisonous-plants-and-plant-parts

www.conservewildlife.org/traps.html

www.wildgoose.com/director.htm

www.slideshare.net/rangevein92/fishing-for-food-what-are-the-best-fish-to-eat

www.first-nature.com/fungi/facts/poisonous.php

FURTHER READING

Angier, Bradford. *How to Stay Alive in the Woods: A Complete Guide to Food, Shelter and Self-Preservation Anywhere*. New York: Black Dog & Leventhal, 2001.

Bourne, Wade. *Basic Fishing: A Beginner's Guide*. New York: Skyhorse Publishing, 2011.

Davenport, Gregory J. *Wilderness Survival: 2nd Edition*. Mechanicsburg, PA: Stackpole Books, 2006.

Spencer, Jim. *Guide to Trapping*. Mechanicsburg, PA: Stackpole Books, 2007.

Stillwell, Alexander. *The Encyclopedia of Survival Techniques*. New York: Lyons Press, 2000.

Turner, Nancy J. and Patrick von Aderkas. *The North American Guide to Common Poisonous Plants and Mushrooms*. Portland, Oregon: Timber Press, Inc., 2009.

Wiseman, John. *SAS Survival Handbook, Revised Edition: For Any Climate, in Any Situation*. New York: William Morrow Paperbacks, 2009.

ABOUT THE AUTHOR

Patrick Wilson was educated at Marlborough College, Wiltshire and studied history at Manchester University. He was a member of the Officer Training Corps, and for the past seven years he has been heavily involved in training young people in the art of survival on Combined Cadet Force (CCF) and Duke of Edinburgh Courses. He has taught history at St. Edward's School, Oxford, Millfield School, and currently at Bradfield College, in England.

His main passion is military history. His first book was *Dunkirk—From Disaster to Deliverance* (Pen & Sword, 2000). Since then he has written *The War Behind the Wire* (Pen & Sword, 2000), which accompanied a television documentary on prisoners of war. He recently edited the diaries of an Australian teenager in the First World War.

INDEX

animals 9–19, 21, 30–31, 50–51, 53, 55–58
antelope 19
auger 27

badger 19
bait 14–15, 17, 26
baited hooks 17, 23–24
baking 51–52, 58
balanced diet 9–10
baneberry 40
barks, edible 35, 41, 55
bears 18, 20
beefsteak fungus 46
birds 10, 17, 53–54, 56
blue-ringed octopus 27
boletes 44
borehole 22, 25
brain fungus 46
bulbs 35, 38
buttercups 42

cattle 19
chanterelles 45
chicken-of-the-woods 47
Chilean Air Force 37
clothing 54, 56, 58
cone shells 27
cooking 51, 53–55

dangers 58
deadfall traps 9, 15–16, 19–20
deadly nightshade 42–43
death camas 35, 41
death caps 47
deer 19
destroying angel 47
diet 9–10
dried fish 27
dry fly fishing 23

filleting fish 25
fires 11, 51–56, 58
fish 9, 14, 17, 22–31, 54
fish hooks 17, 27
fishing 23, 25–27
flowers 35–36, 38–44
fly agaric 48
footprints 13
foxglove 41–42
fruit 9, 17, 36, 38, 41
fuel 55–56
fungus 33, 44–47

giant puffballs 44–45
gill netting 24, 30

grain 9, 37
gums, edible 38
guns 10, 18–19
gutting 24, 57

hares 14
hedgehog fungus 45
hemlock 39–40, 42
henbane 44
horn of plenty 44, 46
hunting 9–10, 12, 20

ice fishing 23
insects 23, 54, 58–59

jimson weed 41

larkspur 43
leaden entoloma 49
leaves 29, 33, 35, 39–42, 44, 51–52, 54–55, 59
locoweed 43
lupin 42

marlin 29
martens 18
mink 18
monkshood 41
mushrooms 33, 45, 47

nets 24, 26
nightshade 42–44
noose sticks 17
nuts 10, 37, 51

oyster mushrooms 45

panther caps 49
plants 8–9, 22, 33–35, 37–39, 43–44, 48–49, 56
poison ivy 40
poison sumac 41
poisonous plants 38–39, 48
polecats 18
porcupine fish 28
Portuguese man-of-war 28
puffer fish 28
pulps 38

rabbitfish 28
rabbits 14, 20, 51
reptiles 20, 54
resins 38
rodents 20, 56

sailfish 29

sap 38–39, 48, 56
SAS (British) 47, 51, 53, 58
seaweed 25, 48–49
seeds 37–38, 56
set lining 24, 30
sharks 26–27, 29
shellfish 25, 54
shoots 27, 35
slugs 21
snails 21, 25, 27
snakes 20–21, 54, 58
snares 7, 10, 12–15, 17–20
spear traps 15, 17–20
spearfish 29
squirrels 14
stalking animals 11
still fishing 23
stingrays 28
stoats 18
stonefish 28
surgeonfish 29
survival exercises 19
suspended snares 17
sweet potatoes 34
swordfish 29

tang 29
tenebra shells 27
thorn-apples 41
toadfish 30
traps 9–10, 12–20, 24
triggerfish 30
truffles 45
tubers 35, 48
tuna 30

Universal Edibility Test 33
U.S. Marines 56
U.S. Navy SEALs 29

vetches 43

water hemlock 39
weasels 18
weeverfish 31
wild cats and dogs 18
wild pigs 20, 54
wolverines 19
worms 21, 54, 58

yellow staining mushroom 47